IT'S EASIER DONE THAN SAID

Create elegant company dinners, superb hot buffets, mouth-watering family meals—all on a shoe-string budget with hours of leisure time to spare!

A boon for working wives and mothers, an answered prayer for harried hosts and hostesses, CROCK COOKERY is the revolutionary new version of delicious old-fashioned kettle cooking—but with none of the work, none of the watching and all of the economical convenience and flavor.

With inexpensive cuts of meat and the right seasonings, Mike Roy shows you how to whip up extraordinary meals that taste as if you've fussed for hours.

Get out of the kitchen and enjoy some of the best dishes you've ever tasted—

CROCK COOKERY

D1008071

MIKE ROY'S
CROCK COOKERY

by Mike Roy
with Don FitzGerald

A DELL BOOK

Published by
DELL PUBLISHING CO., INC.
1 Dag Hammarskjold Plaza
New York, NY 10017
The material in this book is reviewed
and updated at each printing.

Dell ® TM 681510, Dell Publishing Co., Inc.
Reprinted by arrangement with Ward Ritchie Press
Printed in the United States of America
First Dell printing—August 1975
Second printing—January 1976

Table of Contents

Pots and Crocks 7

Soups and Chowders 23

Meats 41

Poultry 75

Vegetables and Fruits 85

Specialties of the Crock 103

Index 119

Pots and Crocks

You can't tell the pots from the crocks and thereby hangs the stew!

I had never been so frustrated in all of my cooking life.

You see, I'd heard a lot about the so-called crock pots but no two comments seemed to match. One person would say that the device was the greatest boon to women since the dishwasher, then this bold remark would be countered by the comment that slow cookers weren't worth the powder to blow them up. I found myself bemused and inclined not to take sides.

Now a publisher and an editor entered the scene. (After some ten cookbooks, I have found that editors are thoughtful, educated, intelligent, compassionate, and understanding. Everybody *knows* that publishers have dollar signs for eyes and cash registers for hearts.) It wasn't exactly a surprise, however, to be invited to lunch by the editor and publisher of the Ward Ritchie Press in Pasadena. After all, we had been through about seven books together.

"There is," they explained, "great excitement about crock cookery and we think you should put a book about cooking in a crock together for us."

We set up the deal. I was smirking inwardly, thinking about my file of more than 3,000 tested but unused recipes just sitting there waiting for publication. Pot cooking cookbooks had to be a breeze!

Little did I know!

As I think back, it was the idea of the whole proposition that attracted me. I thought about all the women in this country who work eight hours every day and then head home to perform culinary miracles with their stoves. I remembered the unending requests for quick-dinner menus and for suggestions of something besides chops and steaks that would be quick yet fit into an average income earner's budget.

The slow-cooking crockery pot seemed like the answer to all these problems. Just think! A woman could throw an economical cut of meat into it along with some vegetables, turn the thing on, and go to work. When she returned home, dinner would be done and delicious.

It sounded like a great idea, so I bought a couple of pots and started researching. That's when the frustration began.

The food that came out of those pots was unbelievably bad. The vegetables were indescribable, and the meat was stringy and certainly no better.

I decided on the spot that I didn't want to write the book.

I called my editor who was thoughtful, compassionate, understanding, etc. No go. "We've already put out the advertising that Mike Roy's book on crock cookery was in the works and would be released in April. You can't let us down, Mike."

I was hooked.

A little voice began to whisper in my ear that this job was going to require a lot of research and testing. At this point, I enlisted the aid of an old friend, Don FitzGerald. Besides helping me in my cooking exhibitions, Don has traveled the world, dined at the finest restaurants, sipped the finest wines, writes for *Wine World* magazine as Food Editor and is generally as qualified as anyone I know in the field of food research.

We discussed the project.

Don bought a few more pots and started testing . . . cooking, that is. I did likewise. Three days later we met for a discussion of our mutual findings. We had discovered the same thing. Neither one of us had found *one* acceptable recipe. The meat invariably was string-like, tough, and overcooked; the vegetables were almost dissolved and tasteless and the gravy was flowing disaster.

What was wrong?

We were following the directions and recipes given to us by each manufacturer for his pot. One would think that a manufacturer would market a product that would at least come close to performing its prime function. It would be fair to assume that qualified home economists had tested the machine and provided suitable recipes.

'Twasn't so. We had independently arrived at the same conclusion. A skull session followed.

I remembered that my mother used to start an old dutch oven kettle in the morning, laden with meat, vegetables, and lovely-smelling spices. The cover would go on, and the kettle would slowly simmer on the back of the old wood-burning stove throughout the day. Never once did she remove the lid. Then came the dining hour. She'd fetch the kettle to the table and only then lift the lid. Out would come one of the most enthralling smells that ever entered my nose. Don remembered his grandmother doing the same thing.

My memory took me back to my training days, and I recalled the lessons on cooking *en croûte*, wherein all the vegetables, sausages, meats and spices were placed in a stoneware casserole and the lid affixed. The lid was sealed then with bread dough, and the entire vessel placed in a slow oven to cook all day. When serving time came, one pried the lid off of the now-hard dough, and, again, that glorious aroma came surging up.

These dishes all had one thing in common. The seasoning had to be done at the outset so that the spices and savories would mingle throughout the long cooking time. I'll touch on this characteristic again and again so you'll "get the message."

Now we had the theory.

As we proceeded, we developed more information about crock cookery.

I'll try to condense it down for you, so you can understand that "electrical beast" that Uncle Harry gave you for Christmas which has been gathering dust on top of the refrigerator ever since.

Old Is New

There's really nothing new about the modern fad of crock cooking. It's actually just a convenient version or the old iron soup kettle or stew pot that sat at the back of my mother's black iron wood-burning stove. One-pot meals were not just popular then, they were a must most of the time as midwestern pioneer families had far too many chores at hand to spend all day in the kitchen. A combination of game, vegetables, seasonings, and faith generally filled the pot at daybreak. At day's end, this mixture provided a hearty and rewarding meal for a tired family.

Not a Magic Pot

The modern electric crock cooker or "slow-cooker," is an excellent home appliance. Indeed, it can be a lifesaver to a busy mother or a working woman. In many cases, it will serve just as loyally and rewardingly as that iron kettle you probably remember.

The crock, however, is not all it's been crocked up to be, especially if you believed all those manufacturers' ads about "one-pot gourmet meals." There are some things a crock just can't cook as well as standard oven or range-top methods. On the other hand, there are things that can be cooked in a crock that would be impossible with ordinary pots and pans. *That's what this book is all about!*

Not a Gourmet Book

Those of you who have collected my other cookbooks know that I'm particular when it comes to eating. Sauces, garnish, and expert chef's technique are my forte. This kind of food preparation takes constant attention and generally lots of handwork and finishing by the chef. Well, that's just the opposite of crock cooking.

In fact, after you start your crock you can't even peek once to check for doneness or to adjust seasoning. Now that aspect alone will frustrate many cooks. Others will find this "forget it till it's finished" convenience just to their liking. The only compromise I can see can be made at the start, by assembling the best possible combinations of foods and seasonings before you pop on the lid and switch the crock on. There's really little that can be done at the end of cooking except to thicken a sauce or chowder or add a little cream or wine.

What is Crock Cooking?

Low-heat crock cookery is very low-temperature, "moist-environment" cooking. It takes place at between 200°F. and 210°F., or just below the boiling point. Since the liquids do not boil, there is little steam and virtually no moisture loss or evaporation. Consequently, there will be far more moisture or liquid left in a crock cooker than in a stove-top kettle at the end of cooking. This is also why the flavor of broths from crock recipes is bland or "watery" compared to conventional cooking broths or liquids. Major seasoning adjustments must, therefore, be considered.

Most crock cookers are heated by electric elements that are enclosed in the sides as well as at the bottom of the unit. This insures even heating and, when coupled with the moist, low-temperature recipe formula, virtually eliminates sticking or burning. The high glaze finish of most crockery cooking vessels also insures against sticking and allows for easy cleaning, especially when used at the Low heat setting.

High-heat cooking with the crock is a different matter. Most units will cook at from 300°F. to 325°F. Those with adjustable dials will cook at much higher temperatures. At these higher temperatures, the crock can be compared to a stove-top stew kettle, though the heating is far superior as it comes from the sides and not just from the bottom. Foods cook in less than half the time of low heat setting recipes. And, since the liquids boil, moisture is lost through steam, broths are reduced and foods can burn and stick. High-heat cooking in a crock is not "go away and forget it" cooking, though the single cooking unit is both handy and reliable. For a single dish, it's far easier to plug in the crock than fire up the kitchen range. The crock is also a very handy server and warming unit at the table or buffet.

Economy

Today, especially, economy is just about as important as good taste. Here's where crock cooking can really prove itself. First, it uses energy economically. Most units cook at Low for about the same electrical cost as a 75- or 100-watt lightbulb. High settings use about the same amount of electricity as a 150-watt bulb. That's far cheaper than the kitchen range. Cleanup is cheaper as there is only one pot to wash.

The food budget will also benefit from crock cooking. Crocks thrive on inexpensive meats, cooking them fork-tender with far less shrinkage during cooking than with other methods of cooking. That means more good eating on your family platter for the dollar. Low-heat cooking also retains vitamins often lost in high-heat cooking. Less liquid is required in most crock cookery and those juices left after cooking are filled with natural goodness.

Easy To Use

Because crock cooking is so simple, it is a perfect cooking method for youngsters learning the art, the older folks or the handicapped. (There are crock recipe books available by at least one manufacturer in braille for the blind.) Certainly a crock is the perfect wedding gift and a handy addition for youngsters off to school or going out on their own. With common sense and very little cooking experience, most anyone can produce successful crock meals.

Use Your Household Electric Timer

If you're going to be gone longer than your crock recipe allows, use a household electric timer to start the crock midway through the day. These are the same timers used to turn on and off house lights. Just fill your crock and set the timer to go on at the proper time. Be sure to back up your time calculation from dinner time. (It's not wise to have the timer turn off your crock at midday and let cooked food sit several hours before eating.)

Crock Quirks

Any new appliance takes a few tries to get the hang of it. Crocks are no exception and, maybe, they offer just enough quirks to make it hard for "old cooks to learn new tricks."

First is the importance of not lifting the lid—not even for just a second. Lid raising releases the moist heat that may have taken an hour or more to accumulate. An additional thirty minutes to an hour may be required to replace it, and that extends the whole recipe's cooking time! It also may have released the little moisture required to finish cooking the food. This moisture will not be replaced. Again, the tested recipe has been unintentionally altered.

Some foods just don't cook the same in a slow-cooker as they do on the stove. Carrots are a good example. In standard stove-top recipes for stew, the meat requires several times the cooking time of the carrots and other vegetables. In a crock cooker, after ten hours of cooking, it is possible that the stew meat is very tender and the carrots are still crisp. Celery, beets, turnips and parsnips are other vegetables which require longer cooking times than meats. Smaller trim or a last-minute cooking on High adjusts this, as the recipes will suggest.

Baked potatoes really aren't baked in the crock, but they cook up tender and fluffy. Much like the microwave cooked potato, they're steamed . . . but let's call them baked anyway.

Seasonings

Probably the greatest difference between crock and conventional cooking is in the taste and texture of the finished dish. As mentioned earlier, it's a whole new cooking principle. Crock-cooked foods are prepared in a closed, moist atmosphere. There is no browning, steam loss, or liquid reduction; in essence, there is no concentration of either matter or flavor, which is the case with both oven and stew kettle cooking. Even a pressure cooker lets off steam.

The resulting food is very moist, often bland to the taste, and not comparable to the same dish cooked conventionally.

Fine. It's the nature of the beast, so what can we do? Many crock recipes (until now) do not require browning of meats or poultry before low-heat cooking. It's an extra step, true, but it makes a big difference in both flavor and eye-appeal. Most of my recipes will recommend browning. You may want to increase the seasonings to your own taste.

Similar problems of excess moisture plagued the housewife thirty years ago when pressure cookers became a fad. One trick that solved that problem was to return the pressure cooker uncovered to the heat and to boil off some of the moisture for ten minutes or so. The same trick works with crocks, and, in several recipes, we combine this reducing procedure with the finishing of slow-cooking vegetables. Use a High setting for this process.

Another neat trick is to substitute dry wine for part of the liquid required. Follow the same red wine for meats and white wine for poultry and seafood rule as in conventional cookery.

Meat dishes, especially those without browning, lack the color and richness of standard recipes, though they will be tender and acceptable every other way. You may want to add a few teaspoons of Kitchen Bouquet, Maggi, or brown gravy extract to the finished juices before serving. These products will enliven the dish's color and flavor.

Thickening

I have yet to find a manufacturer's crock cookery recipe book which gives the proper method of thickening. Their folders and cooking directions tell you to mix flour and water together and add it to the meat juice.

May the Devil take the purveyors of this misinformation to the inner regions of the cook's hell and may they simmer in their own lumpy gravy. Flour and water makes wallpaper paste . . . not gravy. Some suggest cornstarch, but any cook will tell you that after a cornstarch liquid mixture cooks fifteen minutes, the starch loses its thickening properties and the sauce breaks.

So right at the outset, how does one thicken? Use Beurre Manie. The French use this universally Simply mix equal parts of butter or margarine at room temperature and flour and add it to the juices. A piece about the size of a walnut will thicken a little more than a pint of loose juice (if you'll forgive me).

14

Add it as you need it, swirling it into the juice until the thickness suits your own taste.

Another easy way to thicken gravies or sauces, and the one I like best, is to make the following roux:

Roux

½ pound butter or margarine
2 cups flour
1 teaspoon salt
½ teaspoon pepper

Melt the butter in a heavy skillet. Sift flour, salt, and pepper together. Stirring constantly, work the dry mixture into the melted butter. The mixture (roux) should have the consistency of a custard pudding. Let it simmer on Low heat for 45 minutes until it's well cooked. Store in an air-tight jar or can (I make 3 pounds of roux and store it in a Crisco can) in the refrigerator. When thickening gravies or stews, add this roux to the boiling juice a tablespoon at a time until the thickness satisfies your taste.

When Is A Crockery Cooker Not a Crockpot?

With the popularity of crock cooking catching on every day, manufacturers are rushing to the marketplace with a great variety of slow-cookers and appliances with crock, pot, slow and other similar descriptive titles as trademarks to get on the bandwagon. Many of these crocks are very fine appliances, using a heavy crockery or ceramic liner to hold and insure even heating during cooking. With moisture sealed in by a tight-fitting lid and heating elements set into the sides, these are true crock cookers or slow cookers. It is for these units that this book of recipes is intended.

A number of manufacturers have come up with "almost crock cookers" and hot-plate conversions that they call slow cookers that just won't fit the bill. Many are unsuccessfully revised frying pans or deep fryers. Others are attractive pots that sit on a separate heating element.

Take a good look at the line-up before you buy. Various sizes and types may be better for one size family than another. But, more importantly, will it really slow-cook, not stick or burn, be safe for a day unattended, and reward you for your investment? The following comments may help.

Various Models of Low-Heat Cookers

While drawing on the same theory of low-temperature moist cooking, each manufacturer has built a different appliance. A check of the most popular models on the market uncovered a number of variations in heating, control settings, and basic usage. The following comments may help in both selecting a crock cooker or using the one you have most efficiently.

1. *CORNWALL CROCKERY COOKER (4-Quart):* Permanent four-quart crockery pot in a metal enclosure. It has a glass lid with side heat elements and even temperature from top to bottom. The three switch settings are: *OFF, MED,* and *HI.* Use *MED* for Low. A nice sturdy unit with a wider than average crock.

2. *CORNWALL TRAY MODEL CROCKERY COOKER (2½-Quart):* Not really an all-purpose, *low-heat* crock cooker as it is only a small ceramic crock with a glass lid set on an electric hot plate. Its capacity is less than 2 quarts for reliable cooking, and it must contain one cup or more of liquid during cooking or the crock could overheat, dry up, and break. Temperature setting *3* is Low. Use only for ½ quantity in recipes.

3. *CORNWALL TRAY MODEL CROCKERY COOKER (4½-Quart):* A better buffet food warmer and server than a crock cooker, since all the heat comes up from the bottom. Attractive ceramic pot with glass lid. Cooks about 3 quarts, at best, using somewhat uneven heat due to having only a bottom element. Use setting *2* for Low, *1* for Warm and forget high heat cooking. Use normal recipe ingredient volume.

4. *CORNWALL TRAY MODEL CROCKERY COOKER (8-Quart)*: With about 7-quart cooking capacity, it is fine for large non-stick recipes. The bottom heat only may be a problem with this large size on some recipes that require even heat over all. Double basic recipes' capacity, but, because of larger heating area, normal-sized recipes may cook in shorter time. Setting *2* is Low, *3* is High and *1* is Warm. Watch out for sticking on settings *2* and *3*.

5. *DOMINION CROCK-A-DIAL*: This one has a crockery liner in a metal enclosure. Cooking capacity is about 3 quarts with glass lid, side heating elements which provide very even temperatures from top to bottom. Temperature settings include *LOW COOK*, *HIGH COOK* and *AUTO-SHIFT*. Recipe tests suggest maximum times in cooking as this unit cooks at slightly lower temperatures than normal. *AUTO-SHIFT* is a setting that allows the crock to cook the first two hours at High and then switches down to Low. Because of the lower temperatures, on recipes calling for 6 hours or more, the *AUTO-SHIFT* to Low method may be advisable for recipes in this book.

6. *EMPIRE EASY MEAL SLOW COOKER*: Cooking capacity is about 2½ quarts in an aluminum removable pan. Heating is not as even as with a crockery pot. Unit tends to get very hot on the exterior during cooking. Temperature settings are *LO*, *MEDIUM* and *HIGH*. Use *MEDIUM* setting for *Low* heat as called for in the recipes. There is no *OFF*. The plug must be pulled to turn the unit off.

7. *FARBERWARE POT-POURRI*: Models come in 3- and 5-quart sizes with a cooking capacity of 2½ and 4 quarts. It is sturdy stainless steel with fully adjustable temperature controls. Use 200°F. for Low and 300°F. for High. These metal units tend to heat faster than ceramic models, so cooking time is shorter than average. Use minimum times listed or reduce cooking of long-period recipes up to 30%.

8. *HAMILTON BEACH CONTINENTAL COOKER*: Similar to Dominion Crock-A-Dial, except that it has a glass liner in place of a ceramic liner.

9. *CROCK-WATCHER*: Similar to Dominion Crock-A-Dial.

10. *NESCO POT LUCK COOKER:* This 4½-Quart capacity cooker should actually be termed a roaster with a low cooking heat setting. The extra-wide design makes it excellent for meats and large poultry. The temperature control, which will go as high as 500°F., must be set at 200°F. for slow-cooking. Also, the metal lid has two steam vents that must be kept closed. Cooking times may be reduced by 30%.

11. *OSTER SUPER POT:* A multi-purpose appliance, this unit may be used as a slow-cooker, high-heat cooker or steamer and as a deep-fat fryer. The interior is a non-stick material and the outside is aluminum with a decorator finish. Because it is a deep fryer also, heating is very fast. Set dial to 200°F. for Low and 300°F. for High. Recipe cooking times may have to be reduced by as much as 30 to 50% for long-cooking periods.

12. *PENNY'S SLOW COOKER & FRYER:* Same specifications as Sunbeam Crocker Cooker Fryer.

13. *PRESTO SLOW COOKERS:* Available in 2¾- and 5-quart models with actual 2- and 4-quart cooking capacities. Cooking area is of a non-stick material. Use the *HI* temperature setting for Low. Recipe times may have to be reduced as this unit heats very quickly and does not have an accurate position to match the 300°F. High called for in crock recipes.

14. *REGAL MARDI GRAS POT O' PLENTY:* A combination cooker and fryer with a 4-quart cooking capacity. The cooking area is of a non-stick material and the outside is of plastic. Since the heating unit is in the bottom, scorching is possible. It is not a true slow-cooker. It heats fast. Use setting *2* for Low and *3* for High. Times for long-cooking recipes may have to be reduced by 30%.

15. *RIVAL CROCK-POTS:* Available in 3-quart, 4½-quart, and 5-quart models. Heavy ceramic interiors are heated from the side for even temperature control. Units have glass and plastic lids and are enclosed in a metal exterior. Control settings are *OFF, LOW* and *HIGH* with both Low and High checking out exactly correct for the times listed in our recipes.

16. *SEARS' CROCKERY COOKER:* Same specifications as the Cornwall 4-quart Crockery Cooker. Be sure to set control dial at *MED* for Low and *HI* for High.

17. *SIMPSON'S CROCKERY COOKER:* Same specifications as Cornwall 4-quart Crockery Cooker. Be sure to set control dial at *MED* for Low and *HI* for High.

18. *SIMMER-ON:* Same specifications as Hamilton Beach Continental Cooker.

19. *SUNBEAM CROCKER COOKER FRYER:* Unit has a removable 4-quart crockery pot and offers excellent heating from the fryer well in which it sits. Controlling the temperature of the crock is confusing as the red spot indicated is too hot. For Low (or 200°F.), set the dial a little to the left of the red spot, and for High, at 325°F. Cooking times for longer recipes may have to be reduced up to 25% due to the fast heating of the unit.

20. *WARD'S/VAN WYCK SIM-R-WARE:* Glass-lined, 4-quart units have heating elements in the side for even temperature control Lids are glass Cooking temperatures appear to be below standard. Use High for the 200°F. Use Low as called for in the recipes.

21. *WEST BEND LAZY DAY SLOW COOKER:* Here, a porcelain-coated steel pot is combined with a separate heating base. Cooking capacity is about 5 quarts Temperatures inside the deep pot hold constant over long periods of cooking. Set dial at *2* for Low and *4* for High There is no *OFF*, and the plug must be pulled to shut off the heat.

When All Else Fails, Read The Directions
(quote from the wise sage Denis Bracken)

Before You Use Your Crock Cooker

Don't just open the box, plug it in, and start cooking. Find out just what you have first A crock or slow-cooker is a really unique appliance, quite different from what you are used to unless you date back to my mother's heavy, black, iron kettle. Unless you cooked with that kettle, you've never cooked like this before.

First, unpack it and familiarize yourself with all the parts. Some units have crocks that lift out of the cooker; others are one piece with a separate lid. Some have several heat settings and automatic features. Most will have Low, High and Off switches. Some come with permanently affixed cords; others detach from the cooker.

All crocks will have a direction book or folder. Read it first—all of it! Each manufacturer knows best how to clean, handle, and cook in his particular mode. It can differ greatly among different brands. Some units must be filled half full to operate properly. Others can be used to dry-cook. Now is the time to find out the limitations of your unit, not after a recipe failure or damaged crock.

Keep the kids away from the crock cooker. It looks sturdy and may cook at low heat, but the ceramic portion is very delicate. Also, many units heat up enough to cause burns at certain exterior points.

Before You Cook

Wash the interior of your crock cooker with warm soapy water, rinse, and wipe dry. Never immerse the crock in water unless it is the type that separates from the heating unit.

Find a safe spot for your crock while it is in use. It should be flat, away from other appliances or areas often used, and out of the reach of children. Watch out for the electric cord. It should never dangle over a table or sink edge where it could be snagged. If an extension cord is used, be sure it is the heavy duty type that will not heat up.

When selecting recipes for your crock cooker, compare those in this book against similar recipes from the manufacturer. There may be differences in times or methods due to the nature of your particular unit. Use your own judgement and adjust accordingly.

All recipes in this book were tested for crock cookers of from 3- to 4½-quart capacity. All recipes may be cut or increased to fit crocks of from 2½- to 5-quarts. Be sure you do not fill your unit over the maximum cooking capacity recommended by the manufacturer.

We should have one more little talk before we begin. Somewhere back there, midst all that research, I mentioned browning. I think it's the most important part of good crock cooking, and I want to set it out in its own niche to remind you of how important it is.

Most recipes from manufacturers recommend skillet or oven browning in a few meat dishes, but not nearly enough. Too often they will tell you to dust chops or short ribs with flour and place them in the crock cooker, adding liquids, seasonings, and vegetables, in the case of stews. What happens is that the flour turns to paste in the moisture and when cooked, it makes a sticky mess in the bottom of the crock. If you like pasty cubes of stew meat or gooey pork chops, then don't brown.

Browning meats in flour serves two purposes in crock cooking. First, it insures that the meat is sealed and will retain its juices during cooking, even very slow cooking. Sticking is prevented and foods come out looking good and separate. Second, browning helps enhance flavors. In crockery cooking, where flavors tend to be bland to start with, the added richness of browning can be a big help. Foods will also taste more like their conventional cooking namesakes. That's a plus.

This is one place where the manufacturers went a little too far in promising a "one-pot miracle cooker." Even when they suggest you turn the heat to High and brown in the cooker, it will take forever in many units. If possible, use the skillet and get the job done in a few minutes. It only takes another minute to rinse the pan.

A Note About Wines

In our seasoning comments, we mentioned the use of wines as part of the cooking liquid in many meat and poultry crock recipes. Here in California, where these recipes were developed and tested, good wines are an important part of good mealtime enjoyment. California wines have become a must in many households, imparting elegance and taste variety to everyday dining.

Wine can be especially significant in making a one-pot meal something special. A glass of rich California Burgundy or Zinfandel is the perfect compliment to the Beef Goulash or Roulades of Beef. Or how about a soft Chablis or fruity Chenin Blanc with Chicken Chasseur or Crocked Chicken with Grapes. Great!

Those of you who listen to my Southern California radio show know that I get lots of questions about cooking with wine and which wines to serve. Well, long ago I started a love affair with California wine. Today, the variety and quality of California wine is comparable to the best the rest of the world has to offer. And for the price, well, just give me a loaf of bread, a jug of wine, a crock cooker, and thou!

Soups and Chowders

I don't know who gets the credit, but there has to be a special place in Heaven for the cook who first made soup. I don't care even if it's Mrs. Murphy throwing overalls in the chowder. Give the old gal a halo and seat her on the right hand. Blessed be her name.

Once you've made a few homemade soups in your pot or cooker, you'll wonder how you ever got along without it. After all, soups got their start in earthen pots and those big iron kettles that used to hang on a tripod over the coals or swing from an iron crane in the old fireplace.

Slow simmering all day is the way to a great soup, extracting all the flavors and blending them into a montage of aroma and taste unequaled even by the gods on Olympus.

Serve soup with hot, crunchy french bread or hot buttered biscuits. Add a salad and a simple dessert and you have one of my favorite meals.

Be a little creative with the garnish. Don't just serve crackers and let it go at that. A liberal sprinkling of popcorn can do wonders! Some of the dry cereals like bite-sized shredded wheat, or puffed wheat or rice or cheese crackers are crunchy additions on top of a bowl of hearty soup. Sliced hot dogs or crumbled, crispy bacon bits do nicely too. Diced cheddar floats and melts into tomato soup and you've got to have Swiss with your onion soup.

Don't forget that some soups are delicious served cold, especially that potato soup, even though it does come in under a fancy French name.

There should be a word here about dumplings and noodles. Some cooks like to float the dumplings on top of the soup or stew. This has an effect on the whole dish. Flour tends to bleed into the broth, clouding it. As a result, the broth loses much of its eye appeal, and absorbs an uncooked flour taste from the dumplings. Follow the advice of the old chef and cook dumplings and noodles in a separate saucepan. You may use just plain salted water but consommé or bouillon cubes added will give more flavor.

Rice, noodles, macaroni, barleys, and grains do not bring good results to pot cookery. They mash, mush, and cling together in glutinous masses. That's why you'll not find casseroles in this book. They just aren't practical.

And while I'm on the subject of what's not practical in crock cookery, let's mention the idea of baking. Some of the manufacturers will feature a recipe or two for baking breads, and the like. Let's face it: ovens are designed for baking, not pots. The heat medium is not right. If you're trying to bake, use your oven. (However, we had fair success with the so-called steamed puddings. Plum pudding, for example, was edible but not great.)

Incidentally, my criteria for acceptability of a recipe required that the result must come up to my standards of taste, eye appeal, and quality. I refused to insert an item just to prove that something could be done in a pot. A hash in the crock becomes a groveling mass of meat, potatoes and onions. Ah, but a hash properly sautéed and finished in the oven with its crispy goodness supporting a poached egg is a thing of beauty which should not be tampered with.

In short, do the things in a pot that can be done in a pot.

Pot-Au-Feu

2   pounds beef shank
1½   pounds chicken breasts or thighs
4   bratwurst or 1 pound Polish sausage
1   onion
2   cloves
2   leeks (white part only)
1   turnip, quartered
2   stalks celery, chopped
½   head cabbage, cut in wedges
1   bay leaf
     sprig of thyme
5   sprigs parsley
6   whole peppers
1   cup dry white California wine
1   cup beef broth or bouillon

Alternate ingredients in the crock cooker ending with the sausages on top. Pour wine and bouillon over all, and cook at Low for from 10 to 12 hours. Strain off broth, and separate meats from vegetables. Press vegetables through a strainer or sieve, returning the pulp to the broth. Season for salt. Slice meats and sausage, serving a few pieces of each per bowl of rich broth. *Serves 4 to 6.*

Beef and Vegetable Soup

12 to 24 hours, two steps

Step 1

2 pounds beef shank, oxtails, or short ribs
2 quarts water
1 onion, chopped
2 carrots, chopped
2 celery stalks, chopped
1 cup tomatoes, diced
1 cup cabbage, shredded (optional)
2 tablespoons salt
5 whole peppercorns
1 tablespoon sugar
1 bay leaf

Step 2

¼ pound (1 cup) fresh or frozen peas, thawed
¼ pound (1 cup) fresh or frozen green beans, thawed
Kitchen Bouquet

Step 1: Combine ingredients in crock cooker and cook at Low for 12 hours. Remove beef from soup and trim meat from bones. Dice meat and return to soup.

Step 2: Add peas and beans. Turn heat to High and cook covered 1½ to 2 hours, or continue cooking 12 more hours at Low. If a darker broth is desired, brown the meat in a hot oven before cooking, or stir in 1 tablespoon Kitchen Bouquet or brown gravy extract before serving. *Serves 4 to 6.*

Minestrone

¼ pound salt pork, diced
1 onion, sliced
1 clove garlic, minced
6 cups light stock or broth
2 carrots, diced
2 stalks celery, diced
¼ head cabbage, shredded
4 tomatoes, diced
1 zucchini, sliced
1 can garbanzo beans, drained
1 can kidney beans, drained
1 cup macaroni or vermicelli
   salt and pepper to taste
1 tablespoon parsley, chopped
2 tablespoons olive oil
   Parmesan cheese

In a skillet, sauté the salt pork until browned. Stir in the onion and garlic, and continue cooking until onion is golden. Place in the crock with the remaining ingredients except macaroni, seasoning, parsley, oil, and cheese. Cook on Low for 6 to 8 hours. Add macaroni, and salt and pepper. Turn heat to High, and cook for 30 minutes or until the macaroni is tender. At serving time, stir in the parsley and oil. Top each bowl with a sprinkling of Parmesan cheese. *Serves 4 to 6.*

Oxtail Soup

1   disjointed oxtail, or 2 veal tails
½ cup onion, sliced
2   tablespoons butter
6   cups light stock or broth
¼ cup parsley, chopped
½ cup carrots, diced
½ cup celery, diced
1   teaspoon lemon rind, grated
    bouquet garni (thyme, marjoram, and basil)
2   tablespoons flour
2   tablespoons butter
    Sherry or Madeira

Brown the oxtails and onion in butter. Combine in crock cooker with the stock and the rest of the ingredients, except flour, butter and wine. Cook at Low for 6 to 8 hours, or until meat is tender. Strain off broth and spoon out excess fat. Return broth to crock along with meat and vegetables. Discard bouquet garni and adjust seasoning for salt. Set cooker to High. Blend flour and butter together and stir into soup to thicken. As you serve, add a tablespoon of wine to each cup. *Serves 4 to 6.*

French Onion Soup

4 to 6 hours

4   tablespoons butter
6   yellow onions, sliced
2   cans beef broth
1½ soup cans water
½   soup can sherry
6   slices toasted French bread, about an inch thick
¾   cup grated Parmesan or Gruyere cheese

In a skillet, melt butter and sauté onions until lightly browned. Pour them into the crock cooker along with the remaining ingredients. Cook on Low for 4 to 6 hours. At serving time, spoon soup into heat-proof cups or ramekins and top with toasted bread. Sprinkle with cheese. If convenient, place cups under a broiler until the cheese bubbles. *Serves 5.*

Chicken Noodle Soup

6 to 7 hours

1 2-pound chicken, cut up
2 quarts water
1 tablespoon salt
1 teaspoon monosodium glutamate (MSG) or Accent
¼ teaspoon pepper
1 leek (white part only) or 1 onion, chopped
1 carrot, chopped
2 stalks celery, chopped
¼ cup parsley, chopped
½ teaspoon marjoram or basil
1 bay leaf
1 6-ounce package noodles

Place all ingredients (except noodles) in the crock. Cover and cook on Low for 5 to 6 hours. Remove chicken parts and bay leaf from pot. Trim meat from bones, dice, and return to broth, along with the noodles. Cook an hour longer or until noodles are done. (Noodles will cook in 20 to 30 minutes on High heat setting.) *Serves 6.*

Variation: Use turkey parts or the leftover carcass of a roasted turkey in place of chicken. One cup of dry white wine may be substituted for part of the water.

Clam Chowder

5 to 7 hours

¼ pound salt pork, diced
2 leeks (white part only) or 1 large onion, diced
6 potatoes, diced in ¼-inch squares
2 tablespoons green pepper, chopped
3 tomatoes, peeled, seeded and diced
1 clove garlic, minced
1 quart light stock, or 2 cups clam juice and 2 cups water
  salt and pepper to taste
1 teaspoon Worcestershire Sauce
  few drops Tabasco
2 7-ounce cans chopped clams
2 cups half-and-half cream
  paprika

In a large skillet, sauté salt pork until lightly browned. Stir in leeks or onion, cooking until transparent. Combine in crock cooker with all the remaining ingredients, except clams and cream. Cook on Low for from 5 to 7 hours. Increase heat to High, add clams and cream. Cook only until very hot, not boiling . . . about 15 to 20 minutes. Serve garnished with a sprinkling of paprika. *Serves 4 to 6.*

Manhattan Clam Chowder

¼ pound salt pork or bacon, diced
2 carrots, chopped
2 celery stalks, chopped
1 onion, chopped
1 28-ounce can tomatoes
2 large potatoes, peeled and diced
¼ cup parsley, chopped
3 7-ounce cans clams, chopped
1½ teaspoons salt
½ teaspoon pepper
1 bay leaf
1½ teaspoons thyme
dash Tabasco

Stir ingredients together in crock cooker and cover. Cook at Low heat for 8 to 10 hours. Adjust seasoning for salt, pepper, or Tabasco at serving time. *Serves 4 to 6.*

Bouillabaisse

7 to 9 hours, two steps

Step 1	Step 2
¼ cup olive oil	1 pound large raw shrimp in their shells
1 onion, chopped	
1 carrot, chopped	1 pound fresh or frozen fish fillets, thawed, cut in 2-inch cubes
1 clove garlic, minced	
2 leeks (white part only), sliced	
	3 lobster tails, cut in 2-inch pieces
1 1-pound can tomatoes	
2 cups water, or 1 cup water and 1 cup clam juice	1 pound fresh clams (optional)
1 cup dry white California wine	
2 bay leaves	
2 tablespoons parsley, chopped	
½ teaspoon thyme	
¼ teaspoon basil	
⅛ teaspoon saffron	
1 tablespoon salt	
1 teaspoon lemon juice	

Step 1: Combine ingredients in a large crock cooker and cook at Low for 6 to 8 hours. Strain mixture through sieve or strainer, pressing with spoon to retain as much broth as possible. Return broth to cooker.

Step 2: Set cooker to High, and when broth boils, add seafood. Cover and cook only until seafood is done, about 15 to 20 minutes. Broth and seafood may be served separately or together in large bowls. Float a piece of toasted French bread on each serving for garnish. *Serves 6.*

Bean Soup

1 lb. dry white beans
2 quarts water
1 onion, chopped
1 clove garlic, minced
2 tablespoons olive oil
1 ham hock or ham bone, or ¼ pound diced salt pork
1 tomato, peeled and chopped
½ teaspoon thyme
1 tablespoon wine vinegar
  salt and pepper

Soak beans in water overnight and drain. If salt pork is used, sauté it in a skillet until browned, adding onion and garlic during the last few minutes; or sauté onion and garlic in oil. Add to crock cooker along with beans, water, and all other ingredients except vinegar, salt, and pepper. Cook at Low for 10 to 12 hours.

At serving time, stir in vinegar, mash beans slightly, and add salt and pepper to taste. *Serves 4 to 6.*

Split Pea Soup

8 to 10 hours

1   ham bone or hock
1   pound smoked sausage
1   pound split peas, or ½ pound each of yellow and green
      dry peas
6   cups water
1   onion, diced
1   carrot, diced
1   stalk celery, diced
¼   teaspoon thyme
¼   teaspoon savory
1   teaspoon salt
¼   teaspoon pepper
1   cup milk or cream
1   tablespoon butter
1   tablespoon flour
      grated cheese (Cheddar or Parmesan)

Place all ingredients except cream, flour, butter, and cheese, in crock cooker. Cover and cook for 8 to 10 hours at Low. Remove ham bone and sausage, dicing the meat. Put soup through a sieve or strainer and return to the crock along with the meat. Turn heat to High, and add milk or cream. Combine flour and butter, and stir in to thicken. Serve garnished with grated cheese. *Serves 6.*

Cream of Asparagus Soup

1   9-ounce package frozen asparagus, thawed
1   onion, chopped
4   cups chicken stock
1   teaspoon salt
¼   teaspoon pepper
1   cup cream or half-and-half
½   teaspoon Worcestershire Sauce

Combine all ingredients except cream and Worcestershire Sauce in the crock cooker. Cook at Low for 6 to 8 hours. Strain off liquid and return to crock.

Separate asparagus tips and add to liquid. Press remaining vegetable mixture through a sieve or strainer and stir pulp into crock. Add cream and Worcestershire Sauce, and turn heat to High. If thicker soup is desired, stir in 1 or 2 tablespoons each of butter and flour which have been mixed together.

Serve when hot and thickened. *Serves 4 to 6.*

Cream of Potato Soup

2   pounds potatoes, peeled and cut in small cubes
2   onions, chopped
2   leeks (white part only), chopped
¼   cup parsley, chopped
1   carrot, chopped
1   quart light stock or chicken broth
¼   teaspoon thyme
1   teaspoon salt
⅛   teaspoon pepper
2   cups scalded cream or half-and-half
2   tablespoons butter

Combine all ingredients except cream and butter in crock cooker. Cook at Low for 10 to 12 hours. During the last hour, stir in cream and butter. Potatoes may be lightly mashed at that time. Continue cooking only until soup is hot again.
Serves 4 to 6.

Corn Chowder

6 to 8 hours

3   slices bacon, diced
2   9-ounce packages frozen corn, thawed
1   onion, chopped
1   large potato, chopped
2   cups light stock or chicken broth
1   teaspoon salt
¼   .teaspoon pepper
2   cups milk or half-and-half cream
    nutmeg

Sauté bacon in skillet until crisp. Add bacon to crock cooker, fat and all with all other ingredients except cream and nutmeg. Cover and cook at Low for 6 to 8 hours. Add milk or cream and cook 1 hour longer. If thicker chowder is desired, stir in roux (2 tablespoons flour which has been blended with 2 tablespoons butter) when adding the milk. Cook until thickened. Serve sprinkled with a dash of nutmeg.

Serves 4 to 6.

Cock-A-Leekie Soup

7 to 9 hours

6   leeks (white part), cut in 1-inch pieces
1   3-pound chicken, cut up
5   cups hot water
2   cups chicken broth
1   teaspoon salt
¼   teaspoon ground nutmeg
12   prunes, pitted

Place leeks in bottom of crock cooker and top with chicken parts Mix remaining ingredients except prunes and pour over chicken Cover and cook at Low heat for 7 to 9 hours, or until chicken meat is tender. Remove chicken and separate meat from bones and skin Dice meat and return to broth along with prunes Turn cooker to High for 15 minutes to reheat chicken and prunes. Serve with hard-crust bread or dinner rolls. *Serves 6.*

Meats

A crock cooker may be the best friend your meat budget ever had. It's the perfect cooking method for the less expensive or so-called tough cuts of meat. Pot roasts, stews, and short ribs are tender every time in a crock due to the low-heat and high moisture concept of cooking. And, on top of that, there is far less shrinkage to crock cooked meats as compared to conventional stove cookery. That puts more meat on the table for the same money.

There are innumerable rewards to slow cooking meat. Crock cooking retains more of the nutritious benefits of foods. This is especially true with high-protein meat. Seasoning and the blending of flavors from a variety of meats and vegetables in the same crock become a new art. Meat juices from slow cooking make excellent sauces and gravies and are the perfect base for soups. There is a lot to be said for slow cooking meat!

Most of our cooking times are figured within a two-hour range, but meats do come in various grades and degrees of toughness. A recipe calling for 6 to 8 hours of covered cooking at Low may require an hour or two more for very tough meat. Factors such as elevation, electric current fluctuation, and the like, can make a difference.

We've mentioned pre-browning of most meats as advisable. In those cases where it isn't possible, or if a recipe doesn't call for browning, always wipe the meat dry first to remove any particles from butchering. It's also wise to trim away as much excess fat as possible from meat (especially pork and lamb) as there is no place for the fat to cook away in a crock cooker.

Now's the time to try some of those odd but reasonable meat cuts you've never tried before. They probably will be delicious cooked in your crock cooker.

Burgundy Spiced Pot Roast

8 to 10 hours

4   pounds beef rump or round roast
    salt and pepper
2   onions, sliced
3   potatoes, peeled and quartered
3   carrots, sliced
1   cup water
1   package brown gravy mix
½   cup dry white California wine
¼   cup catsup
1   tablespoon Worcestershire Sauce

Sprinkle meat with salt and pepper. Arrange it in the crock cooker with vegetables. Blend the remaining ingredients and pour over meat. Cover and cook at Low for 8 to 10 hours. If thick gravy is desired, remove meat and vegetables from the cooker and drop in 2 tablespoons each of flour and butter which has been mixed together. Cook on High until thickened, stirring often. *Serves 5.*

Beef Goulash

1½ pounds beef, cubed
3   tablespoons oil
1   cup mushrooms, sliced
1   small onion, chopped
1   can tomato soup
¼   cup water
1   bay leaf
½   teaspoon salt
¼   teaspoon pepper
1   teaspoon paprika
¼   pint dairy sour cream

Heat oil in a skillet and brown meat on all sides. Spoon meat into crock cooker, and sauté mushrooms and onion a few minutes. Remove pan from heat. Add all remaining ingredients except sour cream to onions, and stir to blend. Pour mixture over meat and stir together. Cover and cook for 7 to 9 hours.

At serving time, stir a few tablespoons of the cooking juices with sour cream, then stir this cream mixture into the meat. Check seasoning for salt. Serve with hot noodles or rice, and garnish with a sprinkling of paprika. *Serves 4.*

Stroganoff

6 to 8 hours

2 pounds flank or round steak
  salt and pepper
1 onion, sliced
1 clove garlic, minced
1 can mushrooms, drained
2 cups beef bouillon or broth
1 tablespoon catsup
1 tablespoon Worcestershire Sauce
¼ cup dry sherry
2 tablespoons flour
2 tablespoons butter
1 cup dairy sour cream

Slice beef into ¼-inch strips about 2-inches long. Sprinkle with salt and pepper, and place in crock cooker. Mix together remaining ingredients except flour, butter, and sour cream, and stir it in with the beef. Cover and cook at Low for 6 to 8 hours. Set cooker to High, and stir in flour and butter which have been blended together. Stir until thickened. Turn off heat and, after a few minutes, stir in sour cream. Serve with rice or noodles. *Serves 4 to 6.*

Creamy Swiss Steak

6 to 8 hours

2   pounds round steak
    salt and pepper
4   tablespoons flour
    oil
1   small onion, sliced
1   can cream of mushroom or celery soup
¼   cup water, broth, or dry white California wine
1   tablespoon steak sauce

Cut meat into serving portions. Season the meat with salt and pepper, and dust with flour. Heat a little oil in a skillet, and brown meat on both sides. Remove meat from skillet, and brown onion a minute or so. Alternate meat and onion in the crock cooker. Mix remaining ingredients and pour them over the meat. Cover and cook for 6 to 8 hours. Serve with fresh parsley or tomato wedge garnish. *Serves 4 to 6.*

Roulades of Beef

6 to 8 hours

2   pounds beef round steak, tenderized
1   package prepared stuffing mix
4   tablespoons flour
4   tablespoons oil
1   can onion soup
½   cup dry red California wine
¼   cup water
1   tablespoon steak sauce or Worcestershire Sauce

Cut steak into 4 or 6 portions and pound out flat. Divide stuffing and place it on the steaks and roll them up. Secure the meat with picks. Dust the outside with flour and sauté meat in oil until browned on all sides. Place in crock cooker. Mix remaining ingredients and pour over the meat. Cover and cook at Low for 6 to 8 hours. *Serves 4 to 6.*

Variation: German-Style Rouladen   *6 to 8 hours*
Substitute stuffing mix in Roulades of Beef with pencil-sized strips of ham and dill pickle, placing two of each in each steak roll. Meat may be cut smaller, allowing two rolls per serving. Madeira or Marsala wine may be substituted for the dry red wine. *Serves 4 to 6.*

Sauerbraten

8 to 10 hours, two steps

Step 1	Step 2
4 pounds beef rump or chuck roast	½ cup cold water
½ cup cider vinegar	2 tablespoons flour
½ cup California Burgundy wine	1 tablespoon sugar
2 onions, sliced	½ cup gingersnaps, crushed
1 carrot, sliced	
1 stalk celery, chopped	
few sprigs parsley	
1 bay leaf	
2 whole allspice	
4 whole cloves	
1 tablespoon salt	
1 tablespoon pepper	

Step 1: Place meat in a large bowl or a removable crock. Mix marinade ingredients and pour over meat. Cover and refrigerate for 3 days, turning several times.

Remove meat from marinade and wipe dry. Lightly dust meat with flour and, using a large skillet, brown it on all sides in a little oil. Place meat on crock cooker, and pour marinade over it. Cover and cook at Low heat for 8 to 10 hours. Remove meat and strain off liquid. Skim off excess fat, and return 3½ cups liquid to the cooker.

Step 2: In a small bowl, make a paste of the water, flour, and gingersnaps. Stir paste into liquid in cooker, and heat on High until lightly thickened, stirring often. Replace meat into crock, and cook on High for about 20 minutes covered. Remove meat to a heated platter and slice it thinly. Pour some of the gravy over it, and serve the remaining gravy at the table.
Serves 4 to 6.

Saffron Beef

2⅓ pounds round steak, cut into cubes
1½ pounds onions, sliced
1 clove garlic, chopped
  salt and pepper to taste
1 teaspoon monosodium glutamate (MSG) or Accent
1 green pepper, chopped
1 pound tomatoes, peeled and chopped
½ teaspoon fresh thyme or ¼ teaspoon dry thyme
⅛ teaspoon saffron
1 8-ounce can tomato purée
½ cup California Cabernet or other dry red wine
2 tablespoons butter or oil

In a skillet, sauté garlic in butter lightly. Add onions, and sauté them until wilted. Pour mixture into the crock cooker along with the remaining ingredients. Stir, cover, and cook at Low 7 to 9 hours. Serve with rice, noodles, or over toast points. *Serves 4 to 6.*

New England Boiled Dinner

1   3½ to 4 pound corned beef
2   bay leaves
6   whole cloves
6   small potatoes, quartered
6   carrots, quartered
¼   teaspoon pepper
2   onions, quartered
    water
1   small head cabbage, cut in wedges

Stick cloves into corned beef. Place vegetables (except cabbage) in bottom of the crock cooker. Put bay leaf in, and sprinkle with pepper. Place corned beef on top of the vegetables, and add enough water to barely cover meat. Cover and cook for 10 to 12 hours at Low. After about 10 hours, lay cabbage on top of corned beef. Cover and cook 1 hour longer, or until beef is tender and cabbage is done. Remove cloves from corned beef and slice thinly. Serve with mustard and horseradish sauce. *Serves 6.*

Burgundy Brisket

9 to 11 hours

1	4-pound beef brisket
4	stalks celery, chopped
4	carrots, chopped
2	cloves garlic, chopped
1	teaspoon salt
¼	teaspoon pepper
1½	cups California Burgundy or other dry red wine

Brown brisket quickly on both sides in a skillet with a little oil. Place it in crock cooker along with the remaining ingredients. Cook at Low for 9 to 11 hours. Remove the meat from the crock. Spoon vegetables into a blender and purée, or press through a sieve or strainer. Return puréed vegetables to broth. Thicken broth, if necessary, with a little flour and butter mixed together, cooking on High. Slice brisket thinly, and serve with sauce spooned over it. *Serves 6.*

Steak in Beer

2   pounds round steak
½   clove garlic
        flour
¼   cup oil
1 ½   teaspoons salt
⅛   teaspoon pepper
1   onion, chopped
1   cup tomato sauce
1   cup beer

Rub steak with garlic on both sides. Cut into serving portions, and dredge in flour. Heat oil in a skillet, and brown steaks on both sides. Season meat with salt and pepper, and place in crock cooker. Sauté onions in skillet and pour over meat, along with tomato sauce and beer. Cover and cook at Low for 6 to 8 hours. *Serves 4 to 6.*

Beef and Kidney Stew

7 to 9 hours

1½	pounds lean beef
1½	pounds kidneys
2	large onions, sliced
4	shallots or 1 clove garlic, sliced
	salt and pepper to taste
3	cups California Burgundy wine
½	cup tomato sauce
2	cans beef bouillon
	oil

Slice beef into bite-sized pieces. Soak kidneys in cold water for 1½ hours, and cut into ½-inch slices, removing any fibrous parts. In a large skillet, brown onions in a little oil and add the beef. Cook until seared on all sides. Pour meat into crock cooker. Add a little more oil to the skillet and sauté shallots or garlic 1 minute. Mix in kidneys, and stir for a few minutes. Pour into crock cooker along with salt, pepper, wine, tomato sauce, and bouillon. Cover and cook on Low for 7 to 9 hours. *Serves 4 to 6.*

Golfer's Beef Stew

8 to 10 hours

2 pounds beef stew meat, cut in chunks
1 can cream of mushroom soup
1 can cream of celery soup
1 package dried onion soup mix
1 cup California Burgundy wine

Stir ingredients together in crock cooker. Cover and cook at Low for 9 to 10 hours. Serve with hot rice or noodles.
Serves 4 to 6.

Souper Short Ribs

6 to 8 hours

3 to 4 pounds lean short ribs
3 tablespoons flour
3 tablespoons oil
1 package onion soup mix
1 cup dry red California wine or water

Dust short ribs with flour and place them in a large skillet. Brown ribs on all sides in oil, and put them in the bottom of crock cooker. Stir together the wine and soup mix. Spoon this seasoning mix over meat, so that each piece is coated. Cover and cook at Low for 6 to 8 hours. Remove meat to a warm platter, and skim off any excess fat from cooking liquid. Thicken with roux and serve as gravy on the side, if desired. *Serves 4 to 6.*

Tijuana Pie

1½ pounds ground beef
1 onion chopped
1 clove garlic, minced
1 teaspoon salt
¼ teaspoon pepper
¾ pound Cheddar cheese, grated
1 10-ounce can enchilada sauce
1 8-ounce can tomato sauce
2 16-ounce cans chili-seasoned beans
1 16-ounce can corn drained
1 6-ounce can pitted olives, drained
6 corn tortillas

Brown beef, onion and garlic in skillet. Pour off excess fat and season with salt and pepper. Wipe inside of crock with oil. Place a tortilla in the bottom of the pot and spoon some of the meat mixture onto it with a little sauce and cheese. Top with another tortilla and layer on a bean cheese and corn section. Drop in a few olives. Continue layers of filling, sauce, cheese, and olives, finishing with a cheese and olive top.

Cover and cook at Low heat for 5 to 7 hours. Serve with additional hot tortillas. *Serves 8 to 10.*

Variations: Add chorizo sausage, canned green chili peppers or substitute stuffed green olives for black olives. Make with cooked chicken or turkey instead of beef.

Pepper Steak

6 to 8 hours

1½ pounds round steak, cut in serving portions
   salt and pepper
2 tablespoons flour
2 tablespoons oil
½ cup canned green chili peppers, diced
1 medium onion, sliced
1 clove garlic, crushed
1 can condensed tomato soup
1 cup water
1 tablespoon lemon juice

Season meat with salt and pepper and dust with flour. Heat oil in a skillet and brown meat on both sides. Alternate layers of meat, pepper, and onion in crock cooker. Combine remaining ingredients and pour over meat. Cover and cook at Low heat for 6 to 8 hours. *Serves 4 to 6.*

Swiss Steak with Vegetables

6 to 8 hours

1½ pounds round steak, cut in serving portions
    salt and pepper
¼   cup flour
2   tablespoons oil
4   carrots, cut in 2-inch pieces
4   medium potatoes, quartered
1   onion, sliced
1   can condensed onion soup
½   cup water
1   tablespoon parsley, chopped

Season steak with salt and pepper and dust with flour. In a skillet, brown meat in oil on both sides. Place vegetables in bottom of crock cooker with meat on top. Mix soup and water and pour over meat. Cover and cook at Low heat for 6 to 8 hours. Serve with parsley garnish. *Serves 4 to 6.*

Corned Beef and Cabbage

10 to 12 hours

1 3 to 4-pound corned beef
2 cups water
½ cup brown sugar
¼ teaspoon ground cloves
1 teaspoon pickling spice
1 teaspoon dry mustard
1 teaspoon horseradish
1 onion, chopped
1 bay leaf
1 head cabbage

Place corned beef in the crock cooker. Mix together the water and all ingredients except cabbage. Pour mixture over meat. Cover and cook at Low for 10 to 12 hours. Remove corned beef and keep it warm. Strain juice, and return it to the cooker along with the cabbage which has been cut in wedges. Cover and cook on High for 20 to 30 minutes, or until the cabbage is done. *Serves 6.*

Beef Tongue with Cranberry Sauce

10 to 12 hours, two steps

Step 1		**Step 2**	
1	3-4 pound beef tongue	1	cup sugar
2	quarts water	1	cup water
1	carrot, chopped	2	cups fresh cranberries
2	onions, chopped	1	lemon, sliced
3	stalks celery, chopped	1	teaspoon nutmeg
1½	teaspoons salt	½	teaspoon ground cloves
2	bay leaves		

Step 1: Place tongue in crock cooker, and arrange vegetables around it. Pour water and seasoning over it. Cover and cook at Low for 10 to 12 hours. Remove tongue, peel off skin, and remove roots at the base of the tongue. Slice the meat, and keep warm.

Step 2: Boil sugar and water together in a saucepan for 5 minutes. Add remaining ingredients, and boil 5 minutes longer. Serve this sauce over the tongue slices. *Serves 6.*

Liver 'n Onions

2 pounds beef liver, sliced
   salt and pepper
½ cup flour
   oil
2 onions, sliced
1 can cream of onion or mushroom soup
½ cup water
¼ cup sherry (optional)

Season liver with salt and pepper, and dust with flour. Heat a little oil in a skillet, and brown liver quickly on both sides. When liver is done, stir onions into skillet a few minutes, scraping to loosen any browned particles. Alternate liver and onions in crock cooker. Stir remaining ingredients together, and pour over meat. Cover and cook for 6 to 8 hours at Low. Serve with rice or noodles and fresh parsley garnish.
Serves 4 to 6.

Beef Liver Steaks

6 to 8 hours

2 pounds beef or calf liver, sliced 2-inches thick
½ cup flour
   oil
1 teaspoon salt
¼ teaspoon pepper
2 onions, sliced
1 1-pound can tomatoes
¼ teaspoon oregano

Combine flour, salt, and pepper, and dredge liver through this mixture on both sides. Heat a little oil in a skillet, and quickly brown liver on both sides. Alternate liver and onion slices in crock cooker. Stir oregano into tomatoes and pour the tomatoes over all. Cover and cook on Low for 6 to 8 hours.

Variation: Add ¼ cup California Burgundy to tomatoes, or substitute prepared spaghetti sauce for tomatoes and oregano.
Serves 4 to 6.

Fruit Spiced Short Ribs

6 to 8 hours

3   pounds beef short ribs
¼   cup flour
3   tablespoons oil
1   can consommé or beef broth
1   cup dried apricots
2   tablespoons brown sugar
2   tablespoons vinegar
¼   teaspoon ground cinnamon
¼   teaspoon ground cloves
¼   teaspoon ground allspice

Dust ribs with flour. Heat oil in a large skillet, and brown ribs on all sides. Place ribs in the crock cooker. Combine remaining ingredients, and pour this mixture over ribs. Cover and cook at Low heat for 6 to 8 hours. Remove ribs and apricots. Skim off excess fat, and serve cooking juices over meat. Top each serving with the cooked apricots. *Serves 4 to 6.*

Crockery Meat Loaf

6 to 8 hours

Almost any basic meat loaf recipe may be cooked in a slow-cooking crock cooker. Be sure that your model is suitable for dry cooking, however. Many bottom-heating units and tray-pot models will not work dry. They may be used, however, with recipes that include adequate sauce to cover the meat during cooking. To be safe, always lightly grease the bottom and sides of the crock before adding meat loaf. Allow 6 to 8 hours cooking at Low, and longer if vegetables such as potatoes or carrots are added on top of meat.

Because some ground beef is more fatty than others, it is best to cook the meat loaf first, before adding sauce. This gives you a chance to pour off the excess fat which will otherwise blend with the sauce. *Serves 4 to 6.*

Parmesan Meat Loaf

5 to 7 hours

2   slices rye bread, trimmed of crust
2   slices white bread, trimmed of crust
1   cup water or wine
1½ pounds ground beef
1   medium onion, chopped
4   sprigs parsley, chopped
3   tablespoons Parmesan cheese, grated
1   egg
1   teaspoon salt
¼   teaspoon pepper
1   8-ounce can tomato sauce
2   tablespoons butter
1   teaspoon oregano

Soak the bread in water, then squeeze out as much liquid as possible. Break up the bread with your fingers, and mix with beef, onion, parsley, cheese, egg, salt, and pepper. Form into a loaf about the size of the bottom of your crock cooker. Grease the bottom and sides of the crock cooker to prevent sticking, and place the meat loaf in crock. Cover and cook on Low heat for 5 to 7 hours. Pour off any excess fat.

Combine remaining sauce ingredients, and pour over meat loaf. Cover and cook on High heat 15 minutes or until the sauce is hot. Serve with an additional sprinkling of Parmesan cheese. *Serves 4 to 6.*

Stuffed Cabbage Rolls

12 large cabbage leaves, whole
1 pound ground beef
1 cup rice, cooked
¼ cup onion, minced
1 egg, beaten
1 teaspoon salt
¼ teaspoon pepper
1 teaspoon Worcestershire Sauce
1 can tomato soup

Drop cabbage leaves in boiling water a few minutes to soften. Remove, drain, and cool. Combine all ingredients except soup. Spoon mixture evenly onto cabbage leaves and roll them up, tucking in the sides before the final end roll, to form a round envelope. Place rolls in crock, and pour the soup over all. Cover and cook for 6 to 8 hours at Low heat.
Serves 4 to 6.

Chili Con Carne

6 to 8 hours

¼	cup olive oil
1	large onion, chopped
1	green pepper, chopped
1	pound ground beef
2	8-ounce cans tomato sauce
¼	cup catsup
¼	cup chili sauce
¼	cup water
1½	teaspoons salt
⅛	teaspoon paprika
⅛	teaspoon cayenne
1	tablespoon chili powder
1	teaspoon Worcestershire Sauce

Heat oil in a large skillet and sauté onion, green pepper, and meat. Pour off excess fat, and place mixture in the crock cooker with remaining ingredients. Cover and cook for 6 to 8 hours at Low heat.

If beans are desired, add to the uncooked mixture one pound can of drained pinto beans and one pound can of drained red kidney beans. *Serves 4 to 6.*

Osso Buco

3   veal shanks, cut in 3-inch pieces
3   tablespoons flour
¼   cup olive oil
¼   cup butter
½   cup port wine
2   tablespoons parsley, chopped
1   clove garlic, crushed
1   lemon peel, grated
3   anchovies
    salt and pepper to taste
1   cup bouillon or broth

Dredge shanks in flour. Heat oil and butter in a skillet, and brown shanks on all sides. Remove pan from heat and place shanks in crock. Pour remaining ingredients into pan, and stir until blended. Pour this mixture over the meat. Cover and cook 7 to 9 hours at Low heat. Remove shanks from liquid, and, if the sauce is too thin, thicken it with a little roux (butter and flour which has been mixed together). Serve shanks on a bed of hot rice topped with the sauce.
Serves 4 to 6.

Veal Scallopini Cubes

6 to 8 hours

2 pounds veal, cut in 1-inch cubes
½ cup flour
1 teaspoon salt
¼ teaspoon pepper
¼ cup oil
½ cup mushrooms, sliced
2 onions, sliced
2 cups brown gravy
2 tablespoons sherry
   salt and pepper

Dust veal cubes with flour, salt, and pepper. Heat oil in a skillet and sauté meat until lightly browned on all sides. Spoon meat into crock cooker, reserving oil in skillet. Add onions and mushrooms to the skillet, and sauté for a few minutes. Pour onion and mushroom mix over meat along with the gravy and sherry. Stir, cover, and cook on Low for 6 to 8 hours. Adjust seasoning for salt and pepper, and serve with rice, noodles, or over toast points. *Serves 4 to 6.*

Spicy Spareribs

3   to 4 pounds lean, small spareribs
    salt and pepper
½   cup sherry
½   cup pineapple juice
½   teaspoon ground cloves
¼   cup brown sugar
1   clove garlic, crushed
2   teaspoons mustard
¼   cup apricot jam

Place ribs on a rack in a roasting pan, and sprinkle with salt and pepper. Place in a hot oven (400°F.) for 20 minutes or so, to render off excess fat. Place ribs in crock cooker. Blend together remaining ingredients, and pour over ribs. Cover and cook at Low heat for 7 to 9 hours, or until meat is very tender. Drain off excess fat, and serve cooking sauce over ribs.
Serves 4 to 6.

Pineapple-Cranberry Pork Loin

8 to 10 hours

1   4-pound pork loin roast
    salt and pepper
1   1-pound can crushed pineapple
1   1-pound can cranberry sauce, whole berry or jellied
¼   teaspoon nutmeg
¼   teaspoon ground cloves

Season roast with salt and pepper, and place in crock cooker.
Mix remaining ingredients, and pour over pork. Cover and
cook at Low for 8 to 10 hours. To serve, slice between ribs and
spoon sauce over each portion. *Serves 5.*

Bohemian Sauerkraut and Sausage

7 to 9 hours

1   quart sauerkraut
2   apples, diced
3   tablespoons sugar
1   teaspoon caraway seeds
½   cup California white wine or water
2   pounds Polish sausage or bratwurst

Place sauerkraut in a strainer and hold it under cold running water. Wash and drain sauerkraut several times. Place kraut in crock and stir into it the apples, sugar, caraway seeds and wine. Cut sausage into serving-size portions and partially bury them in sauerkraut. Cover and cook at Low for 7 to 9 hours. Serve with spicy mustard and horseradish sauce. *Serves 4 to 6.*

French Lamb Stew

2 pounds lean lamb, cubed
3 tablespoons flour
   salt and pepper
   oil
1 large onion, chopped
2 stalks celery, chopped
½ pound fresh mushrooms, sliced, or 1 medium can mushrooms, drained
5 carrots, sliced
2 cloves garlic, minced
2 rutabagas or turnips, sliced
½ cup California red wine
1 can beef bouillon
2 cans herbed tomato sauce
¼ teaspoon rosemary
1 tablespoon Worcestershire Sauce
1 bay leaf
1 teaspoon seasoning salt
1 package frozen peas, thawed

Sprinkle lamb with flour, salt, and pepper. In a skillet, sauté meat in a little oil until browned and place it in the crock cooker. Add all remaining ingredients, except peas. Cover and cook on Low for 8 to 10 hours. During the last half hour, add thawed peas. *Serves 4 to 6.*

Irish Lamb Stew

10 to 12 hours

3	tablespoons oil
2	pounds lamb, cubed
1½	teaspoons salt
¼	teaspoon pepper
3	cups beef bouillon or broth
2	carrots, sliced
2	onions, sliced
4	medium potatoes, peeled and quartered
1	bay leaf
¼	teaspoon marjoram
¼	teaspoon thyme
1	package frozen peas, thawed
2	teaspoons flour
2	teaspoons butter

Heat oil in a large skillet and brown lamb lightly. Pour lamb into crock cooker, and sprinkle with salt and pepper. Add all remaining ingredients, except peas, flour, and butter. Cover and cook at Low for 10 to 12 hours. Add peas during last 30 minutes of cooking.

At serving time, turn cooker to High and stir in flour and butter which has been mixed together to thicken gravy. Cook only to the boiling point and serve. *Serves 4 to 6.*

Curried Lamb Shanks

7 to 9 hours

3   pounds lamb shanks
    salt and pepper
2   tablespoons flour
3   tablespoons oil
1   onion, chopped
1   teaspoon curry powder
½   cup dry white California wine or water
1   can cream of mushroom soup
1   2-ounce jar sliced pimentos
1   tablespoon parsley, chopped

Wipe lamb with a damp cloth. Season with salt and pepper, and dust with flour. Heat oil in a large skillet, and brown shanks on all sides. Remove lamb from the skillet, and stir in the onions and curry powder. Sauté a minute or so, then stir in remaining ingredients. Place shanks in crock cooker, and pour seasonings over all. Cover and cook at Low for 7 to 9 hours, or until lamb is tender. Serve with noodles, rice, or pilaf, garnished with spiced or dried fruits. *Serves 4 to 6.*

Poultry

Poultry is especially adaptable to crock cookery. It generally cooks faster than meats and often faster than some vegetables, such as carrots, celery, or potatoes. One-pot poultry cookery can draw on many of the world's favorite dishes, such as Chicken Cacciatora, Chicken Chasseur, or New Orleans Creole Turkey Wings. The flavors are as rewarding as the recipes are easy to fix. Let's also remember that poultry is still one of the best main entree buys in the supermarket.

A crock cooker is a swell way to take advantage of economical turkey parts, or, for special occasions, to try game hens.

Because of shorter cooking times, you may want to consider using an electric timer switch to make sure that your dinner does not get overdone.

Chicken Cacciatora

6 to 7 hours

2 to 3 pounds chicken breasts or parts
2 teaspoons seasoned salt
¼ cup oil
1 package spaghetti sauce mix
1 1-pound can tomatoes or stewed tomatoes
¼ cup dry white California wine

Sprinkle chicken with seasoned salt. Heat oil in a skillet and quickly brown chicken on both sides. Remove chicken to the crock cooker, and pour off oil from skillet. Combine remaining ingredients in the skillet, stirring until blended and hot. Pour this mixture over chicken, and cover and cook for 6 to 7 hours on Low heat. Serve over hot spaghetti or rice. *Serves 4 to 6.*

Chicken Chasseur

6 to 7 hours

4 to 6 chicken breasts, or 2½ pounds chicken pieces
1 teaspoon salt
  pepper
  flour
  oil
2 shallots, chopped
12 fresh mushrooms, minced, or 1 small can mushroom pieces
½ cup dry white California wine
2 tomatoes, or ¼ cup tomato sauce
1 teaspoon parsley, chopped
¼ teaspoon tarragon

Season chicken with salt and pepper, and dust with flour. In a large skillet, sauté chicken in oil until it is lightly browned on all sides. Remove chicken to crock cooker. Add shallots and mushrooms to skillet, stirring a minute or so, then add remaining ingredients. When blended, pour sauce over chicken. Cover and cook at Low for 6 to 7 hours. *Serves 4 to 6.*

Bourbon Breast of Chicken

6 to 7 hours

2   whole chicken breasts (4 portions)
¼   cup flour
½   teaspoon paprika
    salt
2   tablespoons butter
2   tablespoons oil
2   tablespoons onion, chopped
2   tablespoons parsley, chopped
¼   teaspoon dried chervil
¼   cup bourbon
1   4-ounce can mushrooms, undrained
1   10-ounce can tomatoes
¼   teaspoon sugar
⅛   teaspoon monosodium glutamate (MSG) or Accent
    salt and pepper

Dredge chicken in flour which has been mixed with paprika and a little salt. Heat butter and oil in a skillet, and sauté chicken on both sides until lightly browned. Stir in onion, parsley, and chervil, and cook a moment. Remove from heat. Place chicken in crock cooker. Combine remaining ingredients, and pour over chicken. Cover and cook at Low for 6 to 7 hours. Serve with noodles or rice. *Serves 4.*

Crocked Chicken with Grapes

6 chicken breasts, or 8 to 10 pieces chicken
4 tablespoons flour
 salt and pepper
¼ pound butter
¼ cup onion, minced
¼ cup chicken broth
¾ cup dry white California wine
1 small can sliced mushrooms, drained
2 cups seedless grapes, fresh or canned

Season chicken with salt and pepper, and dust with flour. Melt half the butter in a skillet, and brown the chicken on all sides. Remove chicken to crock cooker. Add remaining butter to skillet, and sauté onion until soft. Stir in all remaining ingredients, except grapes. Remove mixture from heat, and pour over chicken. Cover and cook 5 to 6 hours at Low. About 30 minutes before finished, place grapes over the mixture. *Serves 6.*

Chicken in the Pot

1   3-pound fryer chicken, cut up
1   cup chicken broth
¼   cup dry white California wine
1½   teaspoons seasoned salt
¼   teaspoon pepper
¼   teaspoon marjoram or basil
4   carrots, diced
2   stalks celery, diced
½   onion, sliced

Place chicken in crock cooker, alternating layers with a few vegetables. Mix seasonings with liquids, and pour over chicken. Cover and cook at Low heat for 5 to 7 hours. Remove chicken and vegetables to a serving dish. Thicken gravy with a little roux (flour and butter which has been mixed together) by cooking at High heat. Serve over chicken or to side.
Serves 4 to 6.

Teriyaki Game Hens

8 to 10 hours

2   or 3 game hens, halved
1   tablespoon soy sauce
2   tablespoons sugar
1   teaspoon powdered ginger
1   clove garlic, minced
2   tablespoons sherry
2   tablespoons oil
½   cup consommé

Sprinkle game hen halves lightly with salt and pepper, and combine remaining ingredients. Brush hens on all sides with marinade, and place in crock cooker, arranging all as close to the bottom as possible. Pour over remaining marinade and cover. Cook for 9 to 10 hours at Low heat. Serve with hot rice. *Serves 4 to 6.*

Herbed Chicken and Shrimp

5 to 6 hours

1   large fryer chicken, cut up
1   tablespoon salt
1   teaspoon coarse-ground pepper
½   stick (¼ cup) butter or margarine
3   small onions, chopped
1   clove garlic, minced
3   tablespoons parsley, minced
½   cup port
1   8-ounce can tomato sauce
1   teaspoon basil
1   pound large raw shrimp, peeled and deveined

Rub chicken with salt and pepper. Heat butter in a skillet and brown chicken on all sides. Remove chicken to crock and sauté onion, garlic, and parsley in the same butter for a minute or two. Remove mixture from the heat, and stir in remaining ingredients, except shrimp. Pour mixture over chicken. Cover and cook for 4 to 5 hours at Low. Stir in shrimp, cover, and cook 1½ hours longer at Low, or 30 to 45 minutes at High. Serve with additional parsley garnish. *Serves 4 to 6.*

New Orleans Creole Turkey Wings

4 to 6 hours

2   to 3 pounds turkey wings, cut up
1   onion, sliced
1   bell pepper, sliced
1   can tomato soup
1   garlic clove, crushed
½   teaspoon salt
¼   teaspoon pepper
½   teaspoon oregano
¼   teaspoon thyme
½   cup water
½   cup white California wine (optional)

Alternate turkey pieces in crock cooker with onion and pepper slices. Mix remaining ingredients, and pour all over turkey. Cover and cook at Low for 4 to 6 hours. Serve with steamed rice or noodles. *Serves 4 to 6.*

Variations: Substitute other turkey parts for wings or use chicken wings or chicken parts.

Vegetables and Fruits

For most vegetables, the crock cooker is an excellent cooking method. The enclosed cooker holds in natural moisture and flavors and nothing is wasted "down the drain." Rules for cooking vegetables vary greatly. Some vegetables cook relatively fast and, because they tend to loose color and character after long periods of cooking, are best cooked at the High temperature setting.

When vegetables are combined with meats and poultry, be sure that they are at the bottom of the crock so that they cook in liquid. Trim is important as larger sections or whole vegetables take far longer to cook than smaller pieces. Check recipe instructions carefully.

Most vegetables need no attention during crock cooking and may be cooked ahead, and stored in the refrigerator to be reheated when needed. Precooked vegetables, such as celery, carrots, asparagus, or broccoli, are great as salad ingredients or served by themselves in a vinaigrette dressing.

Fruits are simply delicious in the pot. Fresh fruits, of course, are wonderful (and short time) items, but the dried fruits, such as apples, apricots, and peaches are unsurpassed. You'll have to watch the sugar and the liquid. Also, try a little port or orange liqueur with them. Grated lemon peel helps, too.

Fresh and Frozen Vegetables

2 to 4 hours

Very long cooking of vegetables is unwise. Cook them covered on High for 2 to 4 hours. You must use at least two 10-ounce packages of frozen vegetables, or the equivalent in fresh vegetables. Frozen vegetables should be completely thawed. Fresh vegetables should be washed and trimmed. They cook best if cut into uniform serving-size pieces. For most vegetables, add ½ cup water and stir occasionally. Season to taste at serving time.

Cassoulet

1   pound Northern or dry white beans
6   cups water
1   pound lamb, cut in one-inch cubes
¼   pound salt pork, cut in ½-inch cubes
1   onion, chopped
1   clove garlic, chopped
¼   cup tomato paste
¼   cup dry white California wine
¼   cup water
1   teaspoon salt
¼   teaspoon pepper
½   teaspoon thyme
1   bay leaf
½   pound smoked sausage or Polish sausage
    Parmesan cheese or breadcrumbs

Soak beans overnight, or at least 6 hours. Drain beans and place them in crock cooker with water. Cover and cook at Low heat for 6 hours, or on High heat for 2 to 3 hours, or until beans are tender but not mushy. Drain beans, reserving the liquid. In a large skillet, sauté salt pork until fat coats the bottom of the pan. Add lamb, and stir until browned on all sides. Stir in onion and garlic, and cook until they brown. Remove from heat, and stir in all ingredients except sausage. Into the crock cooker, spoon a layer of beans, then a layer of meat and seasonings, repeating several times and ending with a bean layer. Pour about ½ cup of the reserved bean liquid over the mixture. Cover and cook at Low heat for 10 to 12 hours, or overnight. An hour before serving, cut sausage into ½-inch slices and stir them gently into the beans. Cover and finish cooking. If beans seem dry, stir in a little more of the bean liquid. At serving time, sprinkle the top of the beans with breadcrumbs or a little Parmesan cheese. Serve in bowls with lots of crusty French bread. *Serves 4 to 6.*

Ham Hocks and Lima Beans

8 to 10 hours

1   pound dry lima beans
2   ham hocks
1   onion, chopped
1   teaspoon dry mustard
1   teaspoon salt
½   teaspoon pepper
1   bay leaf
1   cup water
1   8-ounce can tomato sauce

Soak beans overnight and drain. Combine beans with remaining ingredients in the crock cooker and cook at Low heat for 8 to 10 hours. *Serves 4 to 6.*

Bourbon Baked Beans

6 to 8 hours

4   16-ounce cans Boston baked beans
¾   teaspoon dry mustard
1   cup chili sauce
1   tablespoon molasses
½   cup bourbon
½   cup strong coffee
1   16-ounce can crushed pineapple, drained
4   tablespoons brown sugar

Stir ingredients together in crock and cook covered for 6 to 8 hours at Low heat. A half hour or so before serving, turn cooker to High and remove cover to steam off excess liquid. *Serves 6.*

Artichokes

2 to 4 hours

Wash and trim artichokes and place them stem-end down in crock cooker. Pour 2 cups water over artichokes, and cook them covered for 2 to 4 hours on High heat. A little salt or lemon juice may be added to the water, if desired.

Drain and serve with melted butter for dipping.

Sweet and Sour Beans

3 to 5 hours

8   slices bacon, crumbled
4   small onions
½ cup brown sugar
1   teaspoon dry mustard
½ teaspoon garlic powder
1   teaspoon salt
½ cup cider vinegar
2   15-ounce cans butter beans
1   16-ounce can green lima beans
1   16-ounce can red kidney beans
1   16-ounce can baked beans

Fry bacon in skillet until crisp. Remove bacon and drain off some of the fat. Separate onion slices and cook in fat until tender but not browned. Stir in sugar, mustard, garlic powder, salt and vinegar. Cover and simmer for 20 minutes. Drain the lima, butter and kidney beans, and combine with the baked beans, onion mixture, and crumbled bacon. Pour into crock cooker and cook covered for 3 to 5 hours at Low.
Serves 4 to 6.

Savory Butter Beans

4 to 6 hours

2 1-pound cans butter beans (dry limas), drained
2 tablespoons onion, chopped
2 tablespoons green pepper, chopped
1 tablespoon butter
1 can condensed tomato soup
1 tablespoon vinegar
1 teaspoon salad mustard

Sauté onion and pepper in butter until soft. Combine with beans and seasonings and pour into crock cooker. Cover and cook at Low heat for 4 to 6 hours. *Serves 4 to 6.*

Stuffed Bell Peppers

6 to 8 hours

4   to 6 medium green peppers
¾   pound ground beef
1   onion, minced
1   can condensed tomato soup
2   cups cooked rice
1   teaspoon Worcestershire Sauce
½   teaspoon salt
    dash pepper

Cut tops from peppers and remove seeds and veins. Combine remaining ingredients with half the soup and spoon into peppers. Grease inside of crock cooker and stand peppers in bottom. Spoon over remaining soup. Cover and cook for 6 to 8 hours at Low. *Serves 4 to 6.*

Tomatoes Rockefeller

4 to 6 hours

6 firm tomatoes
¼ cup (½ stick) butter
1 tablespoon onion, minced
½ clove garlic, crushed
½ teaspoon salt
1 cup cooked chopped spinach
2 tablespoons parsley, minced
⅓ cup dry breadcrumbs

Slice top off tomatoes and with a spoon, scoop out about half the center. Heat butter in a skillet and brown onion and garlic. Remove from heat and stir in remaining ingredients. Spoon spinach mixture into tomatoes. Lightly grease or butter inside of crock and place tomatoes inside, spinach side up. Cover and cook at Low for 4 to 6 hours. *Serves 4 to 6.*

Corn in the Husks

2½ to 3 hours

6 to 8 ears fresh corn with husks
    melted butter
    seasoned salt

Carefully peel husks back from corn ears without removing them. Wash and remove cornsilk. Brush ears with melted butter and season with seasoned salt. Fold husks back, and trim off any excess stalk so that the corn will fit into crock upright, stalk end down. Cover and cook at High for 45 minutes, then switch to Low for 1½ to 2 hours. *Serves 4 to 6.*

Yams and Sweet Potatoes

4 to 6 hours

Yams and sweet potatoes should be cooked in their skins in a crock cooker. Wash them well, and layer them in crock. Add ¼ cup water. Cover and cook at Low for 4 to 6 hours (depending on the potato size). Season and serve as you would baked sweet potatoes or yams, with butter, brown sugar, cinnamon, and honey. *Serves 4 to 6.*

Hard Shell Squash

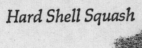

2 to 4 hours

Acorn, butternut, and other hard-shell squash cook in about 2 to 4 hours in most crock cookers set at Low. Cut squash into serving-sized portions, remove seeds, and place in the bottom of the crock, skin-side down. (Dry squash varieties may require ½-cup water to keep them moist during cooking.) Season squash after cooking with salt, pepper, brown sugar, or honey. *Serves 4 to 6.*

Italian Zucchini

2 pounds zucchini, cut into 1½-inch pieces
1 8-ounce can stewed tomatoes
1 clove garlic, chopped (optional)
¼ teaspoon oregano or Italian seasoning
½ teaspoon salt
¼ teaspoon pepper
   Parmesan cheese, grated

Place zucchini in crock cooker, and combine remaining ingredients, except cheese. Pour mixture of ingredients over squash and cover. Cook at High for 2 to 4 hours or until zucchini is just tender. Serve topped with a sprinkling of Parmesan cheese. *Serves 4 to 6.*

Dutch Red Cabbage

3 to 4 hours

1   head red cabbage, shredded fine
4   apples, peeled and sliced
½   cup vinegar
½   cup water
3   tablespoons sugar
1   small onion, sliced
    dash of ground cloves
3   tablespoons butter

Place ingredients in crock cooker in order listed. Cover and cook on Low for 3 to 4 hours. Stir in a little more butter at serving time. *Serves 4 to 6.*

Rancher's Bean Pot

5 to 7 hours

2 pounds link sausages, halved
3 onions, chopped
3 tablespoons flour
¾ cup water
3 1-pound cans pork and beans
1 8-ounce can tomato sauce
1 bay leaf
½ teaspoon salt
¾ teaspoon thyme
1 teaspoon basil

Brown sausages in a large skillet. Remove sausage from the pan, reserving ¼ cup fat. Cook onions and flour in fat, stirring until flour is brown. Remove from heat and pour in water, stirring to blend it with the flour and onions. Pour into crock cooker with the remaining ingredients. Stir to blend. Cover and cook at Low for 5 to 7 hours. *Serves 4 to 6.*

Crocked Potatoes

8 to 10 hours

Use medium-size potatoes, as many as 10 or 12. Wash, prick with fork, and grease. Lay potatoes in crock cooker. Do not add water. Cover and cook at Low for 8 to 10 hours. (This recipe will *not* work in bottom-heat or tray-type cookers.)

Apples 'n Port

3 to 4 hours

4 to 6 cooking apples
½ cup raisins or currants
1 cup brown sugar
¼ teaspoon nutmeg
¼ teaspoon ground cinnamon
⅔ cup port wine

Core apples and cut a score around the sides about one third down from the top. Fill score with raisins or currants, and top with brown sugar, pressing the sugar lightly toward the center of the fruit. Place apples in the bottom of the crock cooker, and pour port over them, seeing that some goes into each apple center. Cover and cook at Low for 3 to 4 hours, or until apples are soft. Serve with excess port sauce poured over apples. *Serves 4 to 6.*

Note: These apples are excellent hot or cold, and especially good served with rich vanilla ice cream or whipped cream.

Cinnamon Rhubarb

- 2 to 3 hours

2   pounds fresh rhubarb
1½ cups sugar
½   teaspoon cinnamon
½   cup water .

Wash rhubarb well and slice it into 1-inch pieces. Place it into crock cooker. Mix sugar and cinnamon together, and sprinkle it over rhubarb, along with the water. Cover and cook at Low for 2 to 3 hours. *Serves 4 to 6.*

Note: This may be the best method of all to cook rhubarb. Rhubarb is so delicate, that stove-top recipes and even oven cooking tends to break the pieces. With the crock, it's perfect every time!

Variation: For a really elegant wine flavor, substitute port for water. Serve as a garnish to lamb and poultry dishes, or spooned over rich vanilla ice cream.

Specialties of the Crock

Let's stress an important point. I have pointed out that you can't use the pot for all cooking. It is not all things to all cooks.

Nevertheless, the pot does have many uses. For instance, the pot is one of the best buffet hot-food servers I've found. It keeps foods like chicken à la king or Lobster Newburg delightfully hot through the course of serving a hot meal. It's an excellent bread warmer and keeper. Appetizers (such as cheese puffs) keep beautifully in the pot. Some of the pots are excellent deep fat fryers, but be sure the one you have is so designed.

I have included several varied items in this section that test exceedingly well. You'll also find several sauces. The spaghetti sauce recipe, I think, is very good. I slipped in a recipe for venison for you game lovers.

For festive events where hot punches are indicated, you'll find the pot without peer. Because the temperature is controlled, you'll not cook the "kick" out of your beverage.

This book will have served its purpose if it inspires you to develop your *own* favorite recipes.

Happiness on you and good cookin'!

Sandwiches from the Pot

Your crockpot is an excellent warmer for hot sandwiches. A variety of meat and cheese-filled bun sandwiches can be made well ahead, wrapped in foil, and refrigerated. Several hours before serving, pop them into the crock cooker. They will be ready to eat in 2 to 3 hours, and will hold for 6 hours or more. It's a great timesaver for parties and for having groups of kids over.

Select your own fillings (such as chili dogs, sloppy joes, minced lunchmeat, or ham and cheese), or try one of our favorites, Crowd Burgers. For dry sandwiches, be sure foil is securely closed. For steamed sandwiches, such as corned beef or pastrami, leave foil loose at top and add ¼ cup water to the crock cooker. Do not use tray-type or bottom-heat units for dry-heat sandwich warming.

Dog Pot

For ball game days, start off with a crock full of hot dogs. They'll hold for hours and be ready whenever anyone wants to build a snack. For a big batch of dogs, drop the wieners into boiling water just long enough to heat. Then pile them in the crock, cover, and set at Low heat. Set the crock in the center of all the fixings and enjoy real convenience while entertaining.

Crowd Burgers

1 pound ground beef
1 tablespoon oil
1 teaspoon salt
½ teaspoon pepper
1 tablespoon mustard
2 tablespoons catsup
2 tablespoons onion, finely chopped
2 tablespoons dill pickle, finely chopped
6 hamburger buns
6 slices processed cheese
  aluminum foil

In a skillet, sauté beef in oil until cooked and crumbled. Drain off fat and season with salt and pepper. Cool. Blend in mustard, catsup, onion, and pickle. Spoon onto bottom half of buns. Top with cheese slice and top of bun. Wrap in 10-inch squares of aluminum foil. Buns may be refrigerated until ready to heat.

Place in crock and cook covered at Low heat for 3 to 4 hours, or until buns are well heated and the cheese is melted. Hot buns may be held at Low for several hours for convenient serving. *Serves 6.*

Cheese-Stuffed Rolls

2½ to 3 hours

8 French rolls
1 pound sharp Cheddar cheese, grated
1 cup stuffed olives, sliced
½ pound bacon, cooked and crumbled
½ teaspoon Worcestershire Sauce

Split rolls almost through. Mix remaining ingredients, and spoon filling into rolls. Wrap securely in foil and heat in covered crock cooker for 2 to 3 hours at Low. *Serves 6 to 8.*

Mexican Cheese Fondue

2 pounds processed American cheese, cubed
2 7-ounce cans green chile salsa
1 4-ounce can green chiles, diced
1 package taco seasoning mix
1 loaf French bread, cubed

Combine all ingredients except bread in crock cooker. Cover and cook for 2 to 3 hours on Low, stirring once after about an hour; or, cook at High heat for 30 minutes or more, stirring often until ingredients are smoothly blended. Set crock cooker to Low for serving. Let guests dip bread through the fondue on long forks or skewers. *Serves 10.*

Shrimp in Marinara Sauce

3 to 4 hours

1	16-ounce can tomatoes
2	cloves garlic, chopped
1	onion, chopped
¼	cup olive oil
2	tablespoons parsley, chopped
2	tablespoons pimento, chopped
½	teaspoon salt
¼	teaspoon pepper
¼	teaspoon basil
¼	teaspoon oregano
	dash Tabasco
1½	pounds raw shrimp
	Parmesan cheese

Drain juice from tomatoes, reserving it. Chop tomatoes and return juice to them. Heat oil in a large skillet, and lightly brown the garlic and onion. Pour remaining ingredients, except shrimp, into skillet, and stir only until mixed. Do not boil. Place shrimp in crock cooker, and pour over sauce. Cover and cook at Low for 3 to 4 hours. Sauce may be thickened before serving, if desired, using a little roux. Serve over rice, spaghetti, or noodles, topped with a sprinkle of Parmesan cheese. *Serves 4 to 6.*

Venison Roast

Most game can be cooked in a crock cooker. It is best to marinate game 24 hours or longer to mellow the flavors. Use my basic game marinade recipe for venison, fowl, rabbit, and other wild game. Select similar cuts of meat in other recipes and parallel cooking instructions. Game fowl, for example, may be substituted for chicken in many of the recipes.

4   pounds venison roast
    Game Marinade (see page 106)
4   tablespoons flour
    salt and pepper
4   tablespoons oil
1   onion, sliced
1   carrot, chopped
1   stalk celery, chopped
1   clove garlic, chopped
½   teaspoon thyme or oregano
1   tablespoon parsley, chopped
1   teaspoon seasoned salt
1   4-ounce can tomato sauce
1   cup dry red California wine, bouillon, or water

Marinate game in a deep bowl overnight or longer, turning several times. Remove game from marinade and wipe dry. Season with salt and pepper, and dust with flour. Heat oil in a skillet, brown meat on all sides, and place in a crock cooker. Combine remaining ingredients and pour mixture over the meat. Cover and cook for 10 to 12 hours at Low heat. The cooking liquid may be strained and thickened with a little flour and butter mixed together for a rich gravy. *Serves 4 to 6.*

Game Marinade

1 cup dry white or red California wine
1 cup consommé or broth
1 cup oil
3 juniper berries, crushed
1 bay leaf
6 peppercorns, crushed
1 clove garlic, crushed
1 onion, sliced

Combine ingredients and pour over game in a large bowl. Marinate at least overnight or up to 3 days for strong game. Turn meat, now and then.

Baked Goods Warmer

Your crock cooker is an excellent warmer and server for many baked goods. Dinner rolls, sandwich buns, muffins, sweet rolls, and taco shells will heat within an hour at the Low setting (covered). Excellent for keeping breads and garlic toast hot for buffet service.

Italian Meatballs in Spaghetti Sauce

4 to 6 hours

Meatballs	Sauce
1 pound lean ground beef	1 8-ounce can stewed tomatoes
½ pound sausage or ground pork	1 8-ounce can tomato sauce
1 cup soft breadcrumbs	1 cup beef bouillon
2 cloves garlic, minced	¼ teaspoon oregano
2 eggs beaten	¼ teaspoon basil
2 teaspoons, Parmesan cheese, grated	1 teaspoon seasoned salt
1 teaspoon salt	¾ cup dry red California wine
¼ teaspoon pepper	
1 teaspoon oregano	
¼ teaspoon basil or marjoram	
¼ cup dry red California wine	

Meatballs: Pour wine over breadcrumbs and then mix all meatball ingredients together. Form into 1½-inch meatballs. Heat a little oil in a skillet and brown meatballs, a dozen or so at a time. Place them in the crock cooker after draining off the grease.

Sauce: Combine the sauce ingredients and pour over meatballs. Cover and cook at Low for 4 to 6 hours. If a thicker sauce is desired, remove the meatballs and reduce the sauce by turning the cooker to High for 15 minutes or so. Stir often. Return meatballs to sauce, and serve over hot, cooked spaghetti topped with grated Parmesan cheese. *Serves 4 to 6.*

Mike Roy's All Purpose Barbeque Sauce

4 to 5 hours

Your crock cooker is the perfect place to make my favorite barbecue sauce. The long cooking blends the aromatic seasonings just right. It's a big recipe because you can use this sauce in lots of ways. As well as seasoning meats, poultry and the like for crock cooking, use it as a hamburger relish, a last-minute cooking and basting sauce, or wherever you use prepared barbecue sauce or catsup. It will keep refrigerated for weeks in a covered jar.

2   onions, chopped
2   cloves garlic, minced
¼   cup parsley, chopped
¼   cup oil
2   8-ounce cans tomato sauce
2   cups catsup
½   cup cider vinegar
½   cup lemon juice
½   cup orange marmalade
½   teaspoon oregano
4   tablespoons frozen orange juice concentrate
4   teaspoons paprika
4   teaspoons chili powder
4   teaspoons salt
    dash Tabasco
2   tablespoons Worcestershire Sauce
2   cups consommé
4   tablespoons sugar

Heat oil in a skillet and sauté onion and garlic until golden. Pour into crock cooker with the remaining ingredients. Cover and cook on Low for 4 to 5 hours. Cool, place in jars, and refrigerate. Spoon over beef, pork, lamb, and poultry when placed in crock cooker. The sauce imparts a rich barbecue taste while cooking.

Creamed Horseradish Sauce

¼ cup whipping cream, whipped
¼ cup horseradish
¼ teaspoon seasoned salt
   few drops Tabasco sauce

Place horseradish in a strainer and allow it to drain thoroughly.
Fold the horseradish into the other ingredients. Serve with
most red meats. A great way to spark up a meal.

Curry Sauce

1   cup sour cream
¼   cup mayonnaise
1   tablespoon parsley, chopped
2   teaspoons curry powder
1   teaspoon lemon juice
½   teaspoon Worcestershire Sauce
¼   teaspoon salt

Combine ingredients and chill. Serve with lamb, pork, and
most other meats.

Peach Chutney Sauce

1   cup peach jam or preserves
¼   cup mango chutney
½   teaspoon Worcestershire Sauce
3   tablespoons sherry

Whirl ingredients together in a blender only long enough to
chop the chutney. Serve with lamb, meats, and many poultry
dishes for added flavor.

Hot Party Beverages

Hot party beverages are a natural for the crock cooker. Whether a spicy, apple-juice drink for the youngsters or a sophisticated and spirited Scandinavian Glugg for the rest of us, the pot will keep it hot and ready for hours. On busy party occasions, start the hot drink off hours ahead of time. It will be just right when the guests arrive.

Decorate your beverage crock with slices of orange or lemon dotted with cloves, or maybe a cinnamon stick. Keep the lid on in between servings to keep the goodness in.

Scandinavian Glugg

2 to 3 hours

2   (4/5-quart) bottles brandy
1   (4/5-quart) bottle sherry, port, or dry red California wine
1   cup sugar
24 whole cloves
12 cardamom seeds
3   sticks cinnamon
1   cup raisins
1   cup unsalted almonds, blanched

Combine all ingredients in crock cooker. Cover and heat at Low for 2 to 3 hours. Serve in pre-heated mugs or glasses. *Makes twenty-five 3-ounce servings.*

Note: Glugg may be preheated quickly on top of the range and poured into the crock for serving. It will maintain proper temperature for hours at Low. Be sure to keep the crock cooker covered in between servings to retain the natural flavors.

Hot Mulled Wine

2 hours

2 cups sugar
2 cups water
4 cinnamon sticks
18 whole allspice
18 whole cloves
¼ teaspoon nutmeg
    peel of 1 lemon
2 bottles (4/5-quart) Burgundy or claret

In a saucepan, combine sugar, water, and spices. Heat until the sugar is dissolved. Drop in the lemon peel and simmer for 5 minutes. Remove from heat, and let stand for 30 minutes. Strain to remove the spices. Combine syrup and wine in crock cooker and cover. Heat at Low for 2 hours. Serve in heated mugs or glasses garnished with a lemon twist. *Serves 24.*

Halloween Cider Grog

3   quarts apple cider or juice
⅔   cup brown sugar
¼   teaspoon salt
1   teaspoon whole allspice
1   teaspoon whole cloves
4   cinnamon sticks
¼   teaspoon nutmeg

Heat 2 cups of the cider with the sugar and salt, stirring until the sugar dissolves. Pour into the crock cooker with the remaining cider. Tie spices in a cloth bag and drop them into the cider. Cover and heat at Low for 2 to 3 hours. Remove spices at serving time. Serve in hot mugs or glasses. *Serves 12.*

Note: For a big kid's kick, add 2 cups brandy to the cider about 15 minutes before serving.

Hot Crocked Tomato Juice

1   46-ounce can tomato juice or vegetable juice cocktail
¼   cup lemon juice
2   teaspoons Worcestershire Sauce
2   tablespoons sugar
1   teaspoon celery salt
¼   teaspoon oregano
1   lemon, peeled and sliced
    dash of Tabasco sauce

Stir ingredients together in crock cooker. Cover and heat at Low for 2 hours, or until hot. At serving time, float a few slices of lemon on top of juice. Serve in hot mugs or glasses garnished with the lemon slices. Add a dash of Tabasco, if desired. *Serves 10.*

Note: At serving time, pour a jigger of gin or vodka into each mug before pouring in the hot juice. You have a Hot Bloody Mary!

Index

SOUPS AND CHOWDERS

Bean Soup, 34
Beef and Vegetable Soup, 26
Bouillabaisse, 33
Chicken Noodle Soup, 30
Clam Chowder, 31
Cock-A-Leekie Soup, 39
Corn Chowder, 38
Cream of Asparagus Soup, 36
Cream of Potato Soup, 37
French Onion Soup, 29
Manhattan Clam Chowder, 32
Minestrone, 27
Oxtail Soup, 28
Pot-Au-Feu, 25
Split Pea Soup, 35

MEATS

Beef
Beef and Kidney Stew, 52
Beef Goulash, 43
Beef Liver Steaks, 61
Beef Tongue with Cranberry Sauce, 59
Burgundy Brisket, 50
Burgundy Spiced Pot Roast, 42
Chili Con Carne, 66
Corned Beef and Cabbage, 58
Creamy Swiss Steak, 45
Crockery Meat Loaf, 63
Fruit Spiced Short Ribs, 62
Golfer's Beef Stew, 53
Liver 'n Onions, 60
New England Boiled Dinner, 49
Osso Buco, 67
Parmesan Meat Loaf, 64
Pepper Steak, 56
Roulades of Beef, 46
Saffron Beef, 48
Sauerbraten, 47
Souper Short Ribs, 54
Steak in Beer, 51
Stroganoff, 44
Stuffed Cabbage Rolls, 65
Swiss Steak with Vegetables, 57
Tijuana Pie, 55
Veal Scallopini Cubes, 68

Pork
Bohemian Sauerkraut and Sausage, 71
Pineapple-Cranberry Pork Loin, 70
Spicy Spareribs, 69

Lamb
Curried Lamb Shanks, 74
French Lamb Stew, 72
Irish Lamb Stew, 73

POULTRY

Bourbon Breast of Chicken, 78
Chicken Cacciatora, 76
Chicken Chasseur, 77
Chicken in the Pot, 80
Crocked Chicken with Grapes, 79
Herbed Chicken and Shrimp, 82
New Orleans Creole Turkey Wings, 83
Teriyaki Game Hens, 81

VEGETABLES AND FRUITS

Apples 'n Port, 100
Artichokes, 90
Bourbon Baked Beans, 89
Cassoulet, 87
Cinnamon Rhubarb, 101
Corn in the Husks, 95
Crocked Potatoes, 99
Dutch Red Cabbage, 97
Fresh and Frozen Vegetables, 86
Ham Hocks and Lima Beans, 88
Hard Shell Squash, 95
Italian Zucchini, 96
Rancher's Bean Pot, 98

Savory Butter Beans, 92
Stuffed Bell Peppers, 93
Sweet and Sour Beans, 91
Tomatoes Rockefeller, 94
Yams and Sweet Potatoes, 95

SPECIALTIES OF THE CROCK

Cheese Stuffed Rolls, 106
Crowd Burgers, 105
Dog Pot, 104
Game Marinade, 110
Italian Meatballs and Spaghetti, 112
Mexican Cheese Fondue, 107
Shrimp in Marinara Sauce, 108
Venison Roast, 109

Sauces
Creamed Horseradish Sauce, 114
Curry Sauce, 114
Mike Roy's All-Purpose Barbeque Sauce, 113
Peach Chutney Sauce, 114

Hot Party Beverages
Halloween Cider Grog, 117
Hot Crocked Tomato Juice, 118
Hot Mulled Wine, 116
Scandinavian Glugg, 115